EARTH SCIENCE PROJECTS
for kids

A PROJECT GUIDE TO
VOLCANOES

Claire O'Neal

Mitchell Lane
PUBLISHERS
P.O. Box 196
Hockessin, Delaware 19707
Visit us on the web: www.mitchelllane.com
Comments? email us: mitchelllane@mitchelllane.com

Mitchell Lane
PUBLISHERS

EARTH SCIENCE PROJECTS ★ for kids ★

A Project Guide to:
Earthquakes • Earth's Waters •
Rocks and Minerals • The Solar System • **Volcanoes** •
Wind, Weather, and The Atmosphere

The author gratefully acknowledges discussions with Dr. Michael O'Neal.

Library of Congress Cataloging-in-Publication Data

O'Neal, Claire.
 A project guide to volcanoes / by Claire O'Neal.
   p. cm. — (Earth science projects for kids)
 Includes bibliographical references and index.
 ISBN 978-1-58415-868-4 (lib. bdg.)
 1. Volcanoes—Experiments—Juvenile literature. 2. Science projects—Juvenile literature. I. Title.
 QE521.3.O544 2011
 551.21078—dc22

                              2010035357

Printing   1   2   3   4   5   6   7   8   9

                                    PLB

CONTENTS

INTRODUCTION

Have you ever wondered what it would be like to experience a volcano's eruption firsthand? Seventeen-year-old Pliny did in the Roman resort town of Pompeii in 79 CE. He began the study of **volcanology** by taking careful notes of the fiery destruction he witnessed that day.

At first, his family saw a tall, rising cloud shaped like a pine tree that looked "blotched and dirty, according to the amount of soil and ashes it carried with it," he wrote in a letter. This was no rain cloud. Soon the wind blew it over the town, where **ash** and pumice stones fell so thickly that they blocked out the sun and made breathing difficult. What Pliny could see through the thick, dark air were "broad sheets of fire and leaping flames" spewing from the volcano, Mt. Vesuvius. Rocked by earthquakes, he saw houses "swaying to and fro as if they were torn from their foundations." Finally, after nineteen hours of erupting, poisonous gases reaching temperatures of over 345°C (650°F) spilled down the mountain and engulfed the town. Though Pliny escaped, historians estimate that up to 16,000 people were instantly snuffed out by the hot, suffocating cloud. Many were buried, perfectly preserved, beneath a thick layer of ash.

Pliny the Younger was not the first person to observe an eruption. Throughout history, world civilizations have thrived in the shadow of volcanoes, walking a fine line between life and death. Minerals and ash left behind by eruptions create fertile soil, rewarding farmers with

Outbreak of the Vesuvius by Norwegian painter Johan Christian Dahl (1826). Pliny the Younger wrote letters about the eruption immediately after witnessing it in 79 CE.

abundant crops. The gorgeous mountain scenery inspires art and poetry. But with volcanoes, one must take the bad with the good. There is always the chance that a sleeping volcano will wake without warning and destroy crops, homes, and lives. Ancient civilizations used myths to understand why—and more importantly, when—eruptions happen. Native Americans, Pacific Islanders, Greeks, Romans, and early Christians explained that eruptions were fits of anger from powerful gods. The word *volcano* comes from the name of the Roman god of fire, Vulcan.

With modern science, volcanologists understand much more about why eruptions occur. Volcanic eruptions happen when **magma** from deep within the earth finds its way to the surface. Volcanoes occur in the **lithosphere**—rock on Earth's surface and just below. The lithosphere floats atop the **mantle**, a not-quite-solid, not-quite-liquid mass of hot, flowing rock. The mantle is over 1,900 miles (3,000 kilometers) thick, but the source of magma that feeds volcanoes is only a thin strip near the crust called the **asthenosphere**.

Six Types of Volcanoes

Fissure volcano: A long crack in the earth's surface through which lava erupts. May form where two tectonic plates pull apart.

Shield volcano: A broad, gently sloped volcanic cone. Created from slow cooling of runny, hot lava.

Dome volcano: A steeply sloped, convex cone. Created from thick, fast-cooling lava.

Cinder cone volcano: Cone-shaped. Erupts with lava and cinders (ashes), which fall on the sides and build up the cone in layers.

Composite volcano: Cone-shaped. Built in layers of lava and ash like the cinder cone, but larger; it has other eruption craters along the slopes.

Caldera volcano: Crater-shaped, like an upside-down volcano. The site of an exploded volcano that has smaller, active craters.

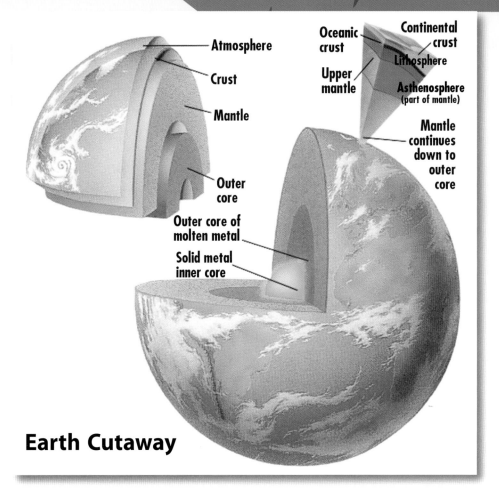

Atmosphere

Crust

Mantle

Outer core

Oceanic crust

Continental crust

Lithosphere

Upper mantle

Asthenosphere (part of mantle)

Mantle continues down to outer core

Outer core of molten metal

Solid metal inner core

Earth Cutaway

In this book, you will explore how these layers interact to form the most powerful places on earth. Conduct fascinating experiments and build working models with materials you have at home to learn more about volcanoes and the forces that shape them. Though simple to set up, each experiment encourages you to think like a scientist, asking questions and providing ideas to take your understanding to the next level. Whether for a school project or just for fun, you'll learn more about volcanology, geology, and science in general.

Many of the experiments need only common materials found around your home. Several experiments use cooking tools and hot liquids. Please ask for **an adult's** help whenever the procedure asks you to. Read each experiment all the way through before starting, and ask a knowledgeable adult if you have questions. Be safe, get messy, and have fun!

Mount Redoubt

MAPPING VOLCANOES

The locations of Earth's volcanoes are not random, but rather are easily explained with the theory of **plate tectonics**. The part of the lithosphere where we live—the hard, thin rock **crust**—is broken into puzzle pieces over the entire surface of the earth. Each puzzle piece is called a **plate**. Many plates are the size of whole continents! Unlike a puzzle, however, the pieces aren't stiff and still. They are in fact constantly moving, carried along like rafts on currents in the asthenosphere.

Most of Earth's volcanoes are found where one plate meets another. When an oceanic plate meets a continental plate, the heavier ocean crust slowly sinks underneath, heading for the asthenosphere. The heat in this new environment causes the oceanic plate to melt. Meanwhile, **fissures** appear in the continental plate from the stress of the moving plate below. Melted oceanic plate material finds its way to the surface through these fissures, creating volcanoes. Volcanoes along the western coast of the United States—such as Mt. Redoubt in Alaska—formed this way.

Likewise, where the plates are pulling apart from one another, hot molten material pours in to fill the gap. Over time, this material forms a long ridge volcano, like the Mid-Atlantic Ridge, which stretches almost from pole to pole through the Atlantic Ocean.

You can see where these hidden puzzle pieces lie by plotting the locations of volcanoes on a map.

Materials
- world map
- package of small label dots or a red marker

Instructions

1. Look up sites of recent volcanic eruptions online:
   Smithsonian Institution's GeoGallery
   http://www.mnh.si.edu/earth/text/geogallery_main.html
   Michigan Tech University: Earth's Active Volcanoes
   http://www.geo.mtu.edu/volcanoes/world.html
   Volcano World—Volcano Activity Reports
   http://volcanoworld.wordpress.com/category/volcano-activity-reports/
2. Using the labels or a marker, place a dot at each site on your world map. If you like, you can note recent eruptions or activity using a red marker and older activity with an orange marker. Plot at least 50 sites, but 100 is even better. The Smithsonian's Global Volcanism Program (http://www.volcano.si.edu/) tracks over 1,500 volcanoes!
3. Step back and look for patterns in the dots you've just drawn. With a pencil, try to connect the dots. Do you see any rings?
4. Compare your results with a map of Earth's plate boundaries, like at the USGS Cascades Volcano Observatory site (http://vulcan.wr.usgs.gov/Glossary/PlateTectonics/Maps/map_plate_tectonics_world.html). What similarities do you notice?

BUILD PARICUTIN, A PAPIER-MÂCHÉ CINDER CONE

On February 20, 1943, a cornfield in Mexico became the site of the newest volcano in the western hemisphere. A crack opened in the earth and rotten-smelling **gases** poured out. Overnight, curious villagers saw the crack grow and build into a mound of **lava** and ash as big as a house, spewing more hot ash and rock. The new volcano continued to grow hundreds of feet every week, reaching a final height of 1,391 feet (424 meters) above the ground in less than a year. The spreading molten rock overtook the village of Paricutin, destroying crops and homes. Luckily, the volcano grew slowly enough that people were able to evacuate.

Paricutin is a classic example of a **cinder cone** volcano. Cinder cones are made from less violent eruptions, where explosions contain thick lava and ash that accumulate to form steep sides on the volcano. You can make a model of a volcano like Paricutin that really erupts!

Materials

- empty plastic soda or water bottle
- cardboard box (approximately the size of a box of printer paper)
- pencil
- ruler
- scissors
- plastic grocery bag
- masking or duct tape
- mixing bowl
- spoon
- 1 cup flour
- 1 tablespoon salt
- newspaper, cut into 1-inch strips
- poster paints
- paintbrush
- clear spray-on enamel (optional)

Instructions

1. Set an empty soda or water bottle against one wall of the cardboard box (wall A). Trace around the bottle's base. To form the cone of the volcano, draw two diagonal lines on wall A, going from the mouth of the bottle to a point an inch (2.5 centimeters) above each corner. Draw a line that's an inch (2.5 centimeters) from the bottom on the other three box sides.
2. Cut the cardboard away along the lines you just made to reveal a cone shape along one wall. Cut out the circle on the floor of the

box. Cover the bottle with a plastic grocery bag and insert it through the hole. The bottle helps give the volcano its shape; the bag protects it from papier-mâché and paint for easy removal.

3. Make supports for your structure by cutting 1-inch- (2.5-centimeter-) wide strips from your waste cardboard. Tape one end of each strip to the low edges of the box; lay the other edges near the top of the bottle. Secure them loosely with tape.

4. Mix papier-mâché paste: stir together the flour, salt, and 1 cup of water. Stir until the mixture is free of lumps.

5. Cover your volcano skeleton with papier-mâché. This step is messy! Do it outside, or with layers of newspaper covering your work surface. Dip a newspaper strip lightly into the paste, using your fingers to squeeze off any excess. Drape the wet strip over the volcano frame. Repeat with new strips until your surface has no holes. Let the volcano dry overnight.

6. When it is dry, you can paint the volcano and decorate it any way you like. Allow the paint to dry.

7. If you'd like to use your volcano many times, ask **an adult** to help you make the surface water-resistant by spraying it with a coat of clear enamel. Allow the enamel to dry.

8. Erupt your volcano using the baking soda and vinegar recipe on page 23.

Kilauea

BUILD KILAUEA, A SHIELD VOLCANO

Shield volcanoes form from hotter eruptions because their lava contains mostly **basalt**. This runny, high-temperature lava allows air bubbles to escape easily and less explosively. Also, the runny lava can flow farther away from the eruption site, creating a flat, wide cone. Kilauea and Mauna Loa on the Hawaiian Islands are examples of shield volcanoes.

You can create an eruptable model of a shield volcano.

Materials
- plate
- small plastic or Dixie cup
- tape
- newspaper
- aluminum foil

Instructions
1. Secure the small cup to the center of a plate with tape.
2. Tightly wad sheets of newspaper and place them on the plate to make a relatively flat layer around the cup. These will support the volcano's walls.

3. Drape sheets of aluminum foil over the newspaper and cup. Tape the sheets together and crimp the foil around the edge of the plate. With **an adult's** help, cut a hole for the mouth of the cup, and tape the foil to the cup's edge to form a tight seal.

4. Erupt your volcano using the baking soda and vinegar recipe on page 23.

Mount Rainier

BUILD MOUNT KRISPIES, A STRATOVOLCANO

Stratovolcanoes form the characteristic tall, wide cone that most people picture when they think of volcanoes. Many famous volcanoes are stratovolcanoes, such as Mt. Rainier in the western United States and Mt. Fuji in Japan.

Stratovolcanoes usually occur at **subduction zones**, where one tectonic plate is plunging under another. The submerged plate melts into the magma that feeds the volcano. This type of magma tends to contain trapped water and air, producing extremely explosive and violent eruptions with lots of ash and thick, **viscous** lava. Strato-volcanoes—such as Mt. St. Helens, Mt. Pinatubo, and Mt. Vesuvius—are responsible for the most dangerous eruptions in history.

Stratovolcanoes produce thick lava that cannot flow far. It hardens on the sides of the volcano, creating a steeply sloping, cone-shaped mountain. Falling ash adds to the deposit. Eruptions tend to be spaced out by hundreds or even thousands of years, such that each eruption makes a new layer of ash and lava on the sides of the mountain. The layers pile on top of each other, resulting in a growing mountain that can reach heights of over 14,000 feet (4,268 meters).

You can make a towering stratovolcano to study how the layers form in each eruption, and to understand how they look as they stack on top of each other. The oldest layers are found on the bottom of the stack and the youngest layers on top, an idea geologists call the **principle of superposition**. Knowing which rocks are oldest can help volcanologists understand what has happened to the volcano over time.

Materials

- 3 tablespoons butter
- 5 cups mini marshmallows
- large glass mixing bowl
- wooden spoon
- microwave
- 6 cups crisp rice cereal (such as Rice Krispies cereal or Cocoa Krispies cereal)
- large plate (9-inch pie plate works well)
- small toys, such as Tinkertoy or Lincoln Logs pieces
- aluminum foil
- semisweet chocolate chips
- white chocolate chips or white candy chips
- small microwavable bowl
- food coloring (optional)
- **an adult**
- sharp knife

Instructions

1. First, make a batch of Rice Krispies Treats. Add the butter and marshmallows to the mixing bowl, and heat in the microwave for 2 minutes on high power. Stir the mixture thoroughly. Return it to the microwave for 1 minute more. Stir the hot mixture until it is completely smooth. Add the cereal, stirring until it is completely coated.

2. When the mixture is cool enough to handle, build a volcano shape on a large plate. If you like, create chambers or vents by building around clean objects that can be removed later—such as Tinkertoy construction pieces wrapped in aluminum foil. If you wish to erupt your volcano, set a Lincoln Logs piece wrapped in aluminum foil in the center of the mixture and form the mountain around it. Set the giant treat in the fridge to harden for an hour.

3. Once the new volcano is solid, create candy layers to simulate past eruptions. Place $\frac{1}{3}$ cup chocolate chips in a microwavable bowl and heat them for 30 seconds at a time on high power, stirring to help the melting process, until the chocolate is completely smooth. Use the spoon to drizzle, pour, and spread chocolate "lava" from the top of the volcano to the bottom. Repeat if you need more lava to cover the volcano's surface, or if you prefer thicker lava.
4. Repeat step 3 with white chocolate or candy chips. Once melted, stir in food coloring if you like.
5. Repeat step 3 with chocolate chips.
6. Remove any non-food objects from your new volcano. If you want, you can erupt your volcano using the baking soda and vinegar recipe on page 23.
7. Ask for **an adult's** help to cut the volcano into wedges, from the top down. As you serve volcano pieces to your friends and family, note the candy layers from the different "eruptions." As the principle of superposition will tell you, the oldest layer is on the bottom; the youngest is on the top.

Old Faithful

FROSTING HOT SPOTS

While most volcanoes occur near the edges of plates, some clearly do not. These oddball volcanoes occur over **hot spots**, fixed places in the mantle that are continually much hotter than the surrounding mantle. The uneven heating starts at Earth's **core** and causes the mantle to bulge upward. As the bulge rises, it sucks up hot, deep mantle material like a straw, sending it toward the lithosphere.

Though the hot spot in the mantle stays put, the crustal plate above it does not. As plate movement carries a hot spot volcano away from the hot spot, it runs out of magma and goes dormant. A new volcano springs

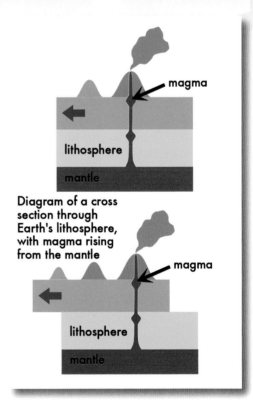

Diagram of a cross section through Earth's lithosphere, with magma rising from the mantle

The Hawaiian-Emperor chain of underwater mountains was created over millions of years as the Pacific plate moved across the Hawaiian hot spot.

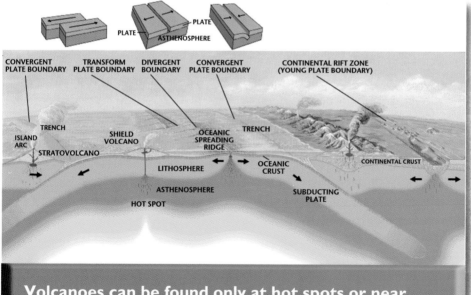

PLATE

PLATE

ASTHENOSPHERE

CONVERGENT PLATE BOUNDARY

TRANSFORM PLATE BOUNDARY

DIVERGENT BOUNDARY

CONVERGENT PLATE BOUNDARY

CONTINENTAL RIFT ZONE (YOUNG PLATE BOUNDARY)

TRENCH

ISLAND ARC

STRATOVOLCANO

SHIELD VOLCANO

OCEANIC SPREADING RIDGE

TRENCH

LITHOSPHERE

OCEANIC CRUST

CONTINENTAL CRUST

ASTHENOSPHERE

HOT SPOT

SUBDUCTING PLATE

Volcanoes can be found only at hot spots or near tectonic plate boundaries. These weak points in the earth's crust allow magma from the asthenosphere to find its way to the earth's surface.

up when the mantle hot spot finds a weakness in the new stretch of crust. The chain of Hawaiian islands were formed this way as the Pacific plate passed over the Hawaiian hot spot.

To illustrate how plate motion affects volcano formation over hot spots, you can make your own frosting island chain.

Materials
- flat cardboard (approximately 8½ x 11 inches)
- aluminum foil
- scissors
- mixing bowl
- electric mixer
- 1 cup powdered sugar
- 2 tablespoons butter, softened
- 2 tablespoons milk
- ½ tablespoon vanilla
- food coloring
- spoon
- heavy-duty zip-top bag
- newspaper
- a friend

Instructions
1. To make a model of the earth's crust, cover a piece of cardboard with aluminum foil. Use a pencil or scissors to poke several holes of varying size through the foil-lined cardboard. The holes should be all in a line.
2. Make thick, rock-colored frosting. Mix powdered sugar and butter together with the electric mixer until smooth and creamy. Add milk, vanilla, and food coloring, mixing until thoroughly combined.
3. Scoop the frosting into a zip-top bag; seal tightly. From the outside of the bag, push the frosting into a corner of the bag away from the zip. Snip off this corner with scissors to create a small hole.
4. Lay newspaper down on the floor or over the surface where you will conduct your hot spot demonstration. Things could get messy!
5. Have a friend hold the cardboard out and flat to represent one of Earth's plates. Hold the frosting bag under the cardboard, aligning it with a hole near one edge. The frosting bag represents a magma plume. Squeeze the bag to force frosting up through the hole, where it will build a frosting "volcano."
6. While your frosting bag stays still, have your friend move the cardboard in the direction of the remaining holes. Your friend can decide how fast or slow to move the "plate." Continue to squeeze

the bag no matter what. What happens when the plate moves slowly? What happens when the plate moves quickly? What do you think happens to the magma when it cannot find a weak spot in the crust?

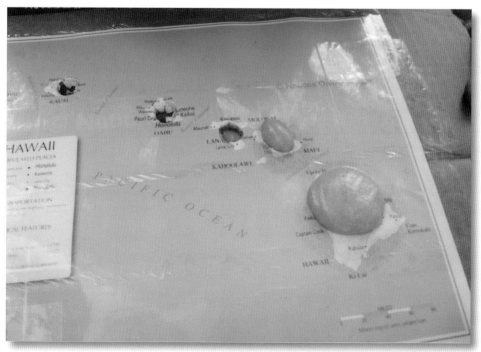

ERUPTION IN A BOTTLE

During an eruption, volcanoes produce lava, **tephra** (airborne volcanic rocks), ash, and gases. Different kinds of eruptions create these products in different amounts.

The following are recipes that cause safe (but messy!) chemical reactions that look just like erupting lava. Like volcanoes, these eruptions are powered by large amounts of trapped gas (in this case, carbon dioxide). Pressure from the trapped gas forces the liquid up and out of its container, much as lava is forced out of a volcano. Use the following recipes either in a 20-ounce soda bottle or in the volcano models you've already made.

Baking Soda and Vinegar
Combine two common household ingredients —baking soda and vinegar—to produce a gentle, foamy eruption. The acetic acid in vinegar breaks down the baking soda's sodium bicarbonate, releasing enormous volumes of carbon dioxide.

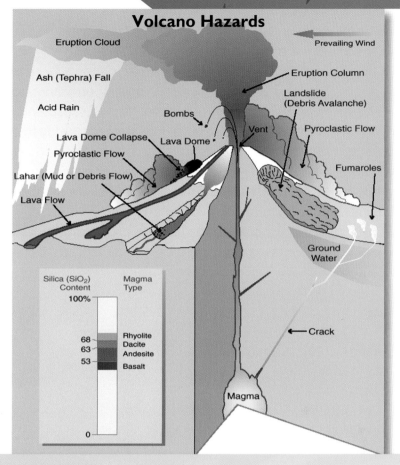

Volcano Hazards

Eruption Cloud

Prevailing Wind

Ash (Tephra) Fall

Eruption Column

Acid Rain

Landslide
(Debris Avalanche)

Bombs

Lava Dome Collapse

Lava Dome

Vent

Pyroclastic Flow

Pyroclastic Flow

Fumaroles

Lahar (Mud or Debris Flow)

Lava Flow

Ground
Water

Silica (SiO$_2$)
Content

Magma
Type

100%

68
63
53

Rhyolite
Dacite
Andesite
Basalt

Crack

Magma

0

Magma

Materials
- empty plastic bottle or volcano model
- baking soda
- vinegar
- spoon
- red food coloring

Instructions
1. Spoon a generous amount of baking soda into the soon-to-be volcano.
2. Add food coloring to the vinegar until it is as red as you like.
3. Slowly pour the vinegar into the volcano container until the eruption begins. Watch what happens.
4. Re-create the eruption again and again by adding more baking soda or vinegar. Keep a notebook of the amounts you add of each ingredient. What amounts of baking soda and vinegar give you the biggest eruption?

Mentos Chewy Mints Candy and Soda

A more spectacular eruption occurs by mixing soda and Mentos Chewy Mints, a popular candy. Carbon dioxide bubbles in the soda are attracted to the rough surface of the mint-flavored candies, encouraging bigger bubbles to grow and creating enough pressure to cause an eruption. Mentos Chewy Mints candies are also dense, sinking quickly in the soda and forming many bubbles throughout the bottle. **Surface tension** is another factor that helps the eruption. High surface tension between the water molecules helps keep the carbon dioxide bubbles under control. Gum arabic, an ingredient in these candies, reduces the surface tension, as does the aspartame in diet soda, creating conditions for bubbles to break free faster.

You will want to do this experiment outside.

Materials
- 3 plastic bottles of any kind of diet soda (any size)
- 3 plastic bottles of any kind of regular soda (any size)
- masking tape
- permanent marker
- pack of original Mentos Chewy Mints candy
- pack of fruit Mentos Chewy Mints candy
- tape measure
- a friend
- stopwatch

Instructions
1. Label the bottles with the masking tape and marker. For each kind of soda, mark two bottles "mint" and one bottle "fruit."
2. Uncap one "mint" diet soda bottle. Drop in four original Mentos Chewy Mints candies, and have your friend start the stopwatch.
3. Watch the explosion and record your observations. Measure the height of the explosion and time how long it lasts.
4. Repeat the experiment with the regular soda "mint" bottle and the diet and regular soda "fruit" bottles. How do their explosions compare?
5. Crush the remaining mint candies into small pieces and make two piles with the pieces. Drop one pile into a diet soda "mint" bottle

and record your observations. Repeat with the regular soda "mint" bottle.

6. Consult your notes to determine which conditions created the most explosive eruption. Repeat these conditions with a model volcano, if you dare!

LAVA VISCOSITY AND FLOW

When it comes to volcanoes, the **viscosity** of the magma—and the resulting lava—determines everything, from how explosive the eruption will be to the shape the volcano mountain will take.

Viscosity is a measure of the density, or thickness, of any liquid. When a liquid is highly viscous, it flows thick and slow, like corn syrup. When a liquid is less viscous, it flows thin and quick, like water. Heating a liquid lowers its viscosity; hotter lavas are runnier than cooler lavas. Even though lava is 100,000 times more viscous than water, it still behaves as a liquid and can flow great distances.

Composition determines a lava's viscosity. Low-viscosity lavas are basaltic, which means they are made of mostly dark-colored minerals and harden to basalt when cool. Basaltic lavas are extremely hot (greater than 510°C, or 950°F), and do not trap gases well—the bubbles simply escape—creating gentle eruptions of lava rivers. The Hawaiian Island volcanoes erupt with basaltic lavas. On the other hand, high-viscosity lavas are **felsic**, meaning they have more quartz and lighter-colored minerals and harden to **rhyolite** when cool. Felsic lavas are cooler (as low as 340°C, or 650°F) and do not travel far. They can trap air, making them prone to dangerous explosions. Catastrophic eruptions, such as Mt. St. Helens in 1980, are almost always caused by felsic lavas.

You can understand more about how lavas flow, trap air, and behave under different temperatures by investigating the viscosity of common kitchen liquids.

Materials
- 4 clean, pint-sized jars
- water
- cooking oil
- dish soap
- honey
- measuring cups
- thermometer
- stopwatch
- 4 pennies
- 4 long straws
- refrigerator
- newspaper
- large cookie sheet
- books or dishes
- small obstacles (blocks, toy cars, small plastic animals)
- tape

Instructions
1. Add 1½ cups of one liquid—water, cooking oil, dish soap, or honey— to each jar. If the liquids aren't already at room temperature, let the jars sit on a counter for a few hours. Record their temperatures— they should all be about the same.
2. Get your stopwatch ready! Drop a penny from the mouth of each jar. Time how long the penny takes to reach the bottom. Do this a few times and take an average to get the most accurate value.
3. Place one end of each straw at the bottom of a different liquid. Gently blow a few bubbles. Time how long the bubbles take to break the surface. Again, do this a few times and find the average.
4. Compare the penny-sinking/bubble-rising times. The liquid with the longest times of the four is the most viscous; the liquid with the shortest times is the least viscous.
5. Move the jars into the refrigerator overnight. The next morning, record their temperatures. Repeat steps 2 and 3 with the cold jars.
6. How has temperature affected the rates of pennies sinking and bubbles rising? Which liquids are more viscous?

7. Lay newspaper down on a flat surface to protect it from the mess you are about to make. On top of the newspaper, prop up one end of a cookie sheet using books or dishes.
8. Pour a little of each liquid from the cold jars onto the top of Mt. Cookie Sheet. Watch them flow down the mountain. Which liquid flows fastest? Which flows slowest? Why?
9. Clean off the cookie sheet and leave your liquids out overnight to warm up. Repeat step 8 with room temperature liquids. Compare their times and what their flows looked like.
10. Repeat step 9, but this time put some obstacles in the path of your lava flow. On the cookie sheet, tape blocks, toy cars, or small plastic animals of different widths and heights. What happens when the liquids meet an obstacle? Do they flow around or over the object? Why? Use objects or make a wall to try to change the path of the flow.

LAVA BOMBS

Many volcanic eruptions actually don't make bright-colored lava flows. The most catastrophic eruptions occur with highly viscous lavas, where trapped gases explode and propel tons of solid particles into the air. These tiny fragments of exploded rock are called tephra. Important classes of tephra include ash (particle diameter less than 2 millimeters), **lapilli** (particle diameter 2 to 64 millimeters), and blocks or **lava bombs** (particle diameter greater than 64 millimeters).

Larger tephra-like lava bombs are too heavy to travel more than half a mile (about a kilometer) from the volcano. However, lapilli can be partially carried by the wind and land quite far from the eruption site. Under the right conditions, volcanic ash can make its way into the atmosphere and travel around the world for years on prevailing winds.

The lava from explosive volcanoes is significantly cooler—as much as 165°C (300°F) cooler—than that

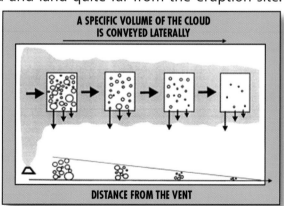

A SPECIFIC VOLUME OF THE CLOUD IS CONVEYED LATERALLY

DISTANCE FROM THE VENT

of gentle, oozing eruptions. Cooler temperatures may leave resistant chunks of minerals unmelted, stuck in volcanic chambers. Combine these chunks with pressure created by particularly gassy eruptions and you have the right conditions for a lava bomb. Even the smallest lava bombs can be ejected from the volcano at speeds of up to 450 miles per hour (725 kilometers per hour), making them lethal projectiles. Lava bombs have been found weighing 30 tons.

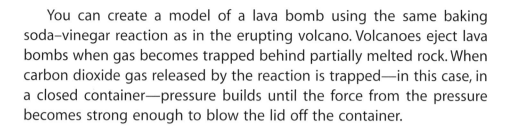

You can create a model of a lava bomb using the same baking soda–vinegar reaction as in the erupting volcano. Volcanoes eject lava bombs when gas becomes trapped behind partially melted rock. When carbon dioxide gas released by the reaction is trapped—in this case, in a closed container—pressure builds until the force from the pressure becomes strong enough to blow the lid off the container.

Materials
- small plastic container with snap-on lid
- baking soda
- vinegar
- spoon

Instructions
1. Place a spoonful of baking soda into a small container.
2. Add 2 teaspoons vinegar. Act quickly—close the lid tightly and place the container upside down on a flat surface.
3. Stand back and watch what happens.
4. Can you change the height, direction, or distance traveled by the "lava bomb"? Try adding different amounts of baking soda or vinegar, or try launching it from a ramp or inclined surface.

Mt. Erebus, a volcano in Antarctica, ejected this 4-foot- (1.2-meter-) tall lava bomb.

VOLCANIC ASH: SMALL PARTICLES, BIG EFFECTS

You probably know what ash looks like from fireplaces or campfires. Volcanic ash looks similar, but is made from tiny pieces of exploded rock instead of burned wood. Under the right conditions, such a small particle can be carried by the wind for thousands of miles (kilometers). After Mt. St. Helens erupted, over 544,000 metric tons of ash fell on the town of Yakima, Washington, more than 80 miles (128 kilometers) away.

When many tons of ash explode high into the atmosphere, the entire earth can literally feel the effects. Such was the case when Mt. Pinatubo in the Philippines erupted on June 15, 1991. It ejected 1 cubic mile (4.2 cubic

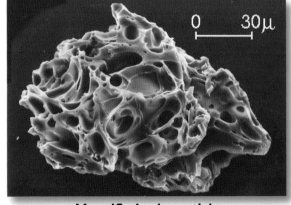

Magnified ash particle

Ash cloud from Mount Pinatubo

kilometers) of dust, ash, and rock up to 22 miles (35 kilometers) high into the air. Winds carried these particles around the globe, where they were able to block out the sun and lower temperatures around the world by 0.3°C (0.5°F). Although this doesn't seem like much, it affected weather patterns around the world, causing floods and loss of crops.

You can observe how a layer of ash can affect ground temperature.

Materials
- 8 identical small paper cups (such as Dixie cups)
- 2 clear plastic sheets (such as a transparency sheet or plastic report cover)
- flour
- 2 thermometers
- sunny spot out of the wind
- clock

Instructions

1. Early in the morning, arrange eight small cups into two rectangles of four cups each. Each rectangle will prop one plastic sheet off the ground.

2. Lay one thermometer flat on the ground inside each of the 4-cup rectangles. After one hour, record the temperature from both thermometers.

3. Place the plastic sheets over the rectangular cup supports. Gently add "ash" to one plastic sheet. Note that ash—wood or volcanic—is **caustic** and easily inhaled. This experiment substitutes flour instead, which has an appropriately small particle size. Spread the "ash" around so as to cover as much of the sheet as possible. Leave your experiment alone to warm up throughout the heat of the day.

4. At 4:00 P.M., remove the plastic sheets and read the thermometers. How are they different? Can you find out why?

IGNEOUS FUDGE

Earth would not be the same without the work of volcanoes. Much of the rocks that cover the earth's surface formed from hardened lava. Volcanic rocks are one type of **igneous** rocks, a class of rocks created from cooled magma (from the Greek word *ignis*, meaning "fire"). Because magma traveled from the hot, liquid-like mantle to the crust very quickly, volcanic rocks formed before crystals had much time to grow. Volcanic rocks therefore have tiny or even nonexistent crystals. One common volcanic rock is basalt, which is used in building.

Basalt

The other type of igneous rock, on the other hand, forms from trapped magma that doesn't reach the earth's surface before cooling. Called **plutonic rocks**, these rocks harden over a much longer period of time, producing a mosaic of large, visible crystals. Granite is a common example of a plutonic rock.

You can explore the difference in formation between plutonic and volcanic igneous rocks by melting and recrystallizing sugar into fudge. You won't need the heat of the mantle. You can make do with a microwave! Most people prefer

Granite

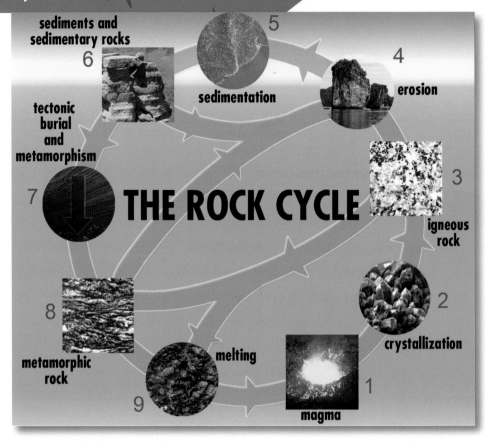

THE ROCK CYCLE

sediments and sedimentary rocks
6

5

4
erosion

tectonic burial and metamorphism

sedimentation

7

3
igneous rock

8

2
crystallization

metamorphic rock

melting

1
magma

9

"volcanic" fudge—small or nonexistent sugar crystals make for creamy fudge. Grainy, "plutonic" fudge happens when sugar crystals have time to form. Ask **an adult** to help you.

Materials
- 12 cupcake liners
- marker
- oven
- refrigerator
- freezer
- 4-quart or larger glass mixing bowl
- oven mitts
- mixing spoon
- $^2/_3$ cup butter or margarine

- 3 cups sugar
- $^2/_3$ cup evaporated milk
- 7 ounces marshmallow cream
- 8 ounces semisweet chocolate (chips or squares)
- 1 teaspoon vanilla
- cookie sheet
- spoon
- thermometer

Instructions

1. Divide the cupcake liners into groups of three. Label the outside of the liners in each group as follows: room temperature (RT), freezer, fridge, oven. Meanwhile, preheat an oven at the lowest possible temperature setting.

2. Microwave butter in the mixing bowl for 1 minute on high or until melted. Stir in sugar and evaporated milk, mixing well.

3. Return the bowl to the microwave and heat for 10½ minutes on high, stopping every 3 minutes to stir well and scrape the sides of the bowl. Use oven mitts—the bowl may be extremely hot.

4. Add chocolate; stir until completely combined. Add marshmallow cream and vanilla; stir until completely combined.

5. Spoon equal amounts of hot fudge into the 12 cupcake liners. Place each group of fudge according to its label—"room temperature" on the counter, "freezer" in the freezer, "fridge" in the refrigerator, and, with **an adult's** help, "oven" on a cookie sheet in the preheated oven. Record the temperatures of each location, if possible. After 1 hour, use oven mitts to remove the "oven" batch. Let them cool.

6. When all samples are cool enough to eat, it's time for a taste test! Which group of the four tasted the smoothest? Which was the grainiest? Why?

GEOTHERMAL POWER: GREEN ENERGY FROM VOLCANOES

Another product of volcanism—the heat from magma rising near the earth's surface—can be harnessed to make **geothermal** ("heat from the earth") **power**. Though the United States gets only 4 percent of its total electricity from geothermal energy, it boasts the largest geothermal plant complex in the world, at The Geysers in California. Smaller countries located on plate boundaries, such as Iceland, the Philippines, and Costa Rica, use geothermal energy to provide 10 to 23 percent of their electricity needs. Iceland additionally uses hot gas directly from the earth to provide 8 percent of its heating needs. Governments around the world are

Grand Geyser, Vent Geyser (small geyser to far left) and Turban Geyser (small bubbly geyser in middle) in Yellowstone National Park

Materials

- empty metal soup can with top removed
- hammer
- small nail (10p weight)
- ruler
- rubber band
- **an adult**
- 3-quart pot
- stove
- heavy-duty aluminum foil
- oven mitts
- toy pinwheel, one blade specially marked (such as with a black line or sticker)
- timer or clock with second hand

expanding their use of geothermal energy, which is better for the environment and cheaper than traditional sources of electricity.

You can demonstrate how a geothermal power station works using your stove.

Instructions

1. Use the hammer and nail to poke two small holes (less than $1/8$ inch wide) on the bottom of an empty soup can, straight across from each other and each about ¼ inch from the edge.
2. You'll need to measure distances over the can once your power station is up and running. Set the can, open-end down, on a flat countertop. Stand the ruler up against it, and fasten the ruler to the can with a rubber band. Make sure the rubber band is tight enough to keep the ruler from slipping when you pick it up.
3. Add water to a 3-quart pot until it is a little more than half full. Cover the pot with two layers of foil, stretching the foil tight over the pot to make a level surface and crimping down around the edges to make a tight seal. This aluminum foil "lid" represents the earth's crust.
4. Poke a pencil-sized hole in the center of the aluminum foil "crust," and set your soup can "power station" over the hole in the crust.
5. Under **adult supervision**, turn on the stove to boil the water in the pot. It will take a few minutes. Keep an eye out for steam to emerge from the "outlets" on top of your power station.
6. Wearing the oven mitt, hold the pinwheel over the steam. Note how fast the pinwheel turns. If you can, try to count the revolutions, or complete spins, the pinwheel can make in one minute. Each time the marked blade completes a turn, count one revolution. This rate of speed is called rpm (revolutions per minute). Note on the ruler how high you are holding the pinwheel. How does the pinwheel's speed change if you move it higher or lower?
7. Turn off the heat under the pot. When the pot is cool, peel back the foil and add enough water to make the pot slightly more than half full again. Replace the foil.
8. Poke holes all over the foil. Return your can "power station" to its original hole. Repeat steps 5 and 6. Now that the steam has more places to escape, how is your power station affected?

40

MEASURING ERUPTIONS

Living near a volcano has its risks, but those risks are much lower now than ever before. Predicting when an eruption will occur is still not an exact science. However, understanding why volcanoes erupt enables volcanologists to make good guesses. Volcanologists use many techniques to monitor changes in certain properties of volcanoes that may signal an imminent eruption. In this way, people living near a volcano can be evacuated early, hopefully saving many lives in the event of a disaster.

Magma Magnetism

Many types of cooled volcanic rocks are magnetic because they have iron-containing minerals such as magnetite in them. When hot, however, the same rocks melt, losing the regular crystal structure that gives them their magnetic properties. At 316°C (600°F), magnetic

Magnetometer

minerals lose their magnetism. The chambers of an active volcano can reach temperatures of over 540°C (1,000°F).

Volcanologists use this knowledge to anticipate volcanic activity. From a safe distance, they can monitor changes in the magnetism of rocks on a volcano's walls using a **magnetometer** (see page 41), an instrument that measures magnetic fields.

Tiltmeter: Eruptions Aren't on the Level!

When magma flows into the main chamber of a volcano, the added material causes the volcano to swell. Just before an eruption, the magma chamber deflates, as hot flowing rock makes its way to the volcano's surface. Volcanologists detect this characteristic behavior—swelling followed by deflating—with a **tiltmeter**. Just like a carpenter's level you may have in a toolbox at home, a tiltmeter can detect changes in height across two or more points on a volcano's surface.

You can build your own simple tiltmeter, and demonstrate how it might react when magma fills a volcano.

Tiltmeter on Mauna Loa

Materials

- table
- 2 pieces of plywood or other flat, stiff board
- duct tape
- 2 small clear plastic containers
- water
- food coloring (optional)
- clear packing tape
- deflated balloon or beach ball
- protractor

Instructions

1. Lay the plywood pieces flat on the table, ends butting each other. Join the seam with duct tape.
2. Add water to two plastic containers until they are half full. Add food coloring if you wish. Place one container on each piece of plywood, the same distance apart from the plywood seam. Secure the containers to the wood with clear packing tape.
3. Gently lift the seam, placing the balloon or beach ball underneath. Slowly and carefully, blow up the balloon or ball a little at a time. Notice how the level of the water responds. Periodically stop, pinch the balloon's neck, and measure the angle between the boards and the table with a protractor. How does that angle compare to the angle made by the water in the plastic containers?

Books

Ganeri, Anita. *Volcanoes in Action.* New York: Rosen Publishing Group, 2008.

Landau, Elaine. *Volcanoes.* New York: Children's Press, 2009.

Lindop, Laurie. *Probing Volcanoes.* Brookfield, CT: Twenty-First Century Books, 2003.

Rae, Alison. *Looking at Landscapes: Earthquakes and Volcanoes.* London: Evans Brothers Limited, 2005.

Van Rose, Susanna. *Volcanoes and Earthquakes.* New York: Dorling Kindersley, 2008.

Works Consulted

Bullard, Fred M. *Volcanoes of the Earth.* Austin: University of Texas Press, 1984.

Cain, Fraser. "Temperature of Lava." *Universe Today*, March 25, 2009. http://www.universetoday.com/guide-to-space/earth/temperature-of-lava/

Camp, Vic. "How Volcanoes Work—The Eruption of Paricutin (1943–1952)." http://www.geology.sdsu.edu/how_volcanoes_work/Paricutin.html

Dunk, Marcus. "Will Krakatoa Rock the World Again? Last Time, It Killed Thousands and Changed the Weather for Five Years, Now It Could Be Even Deadlier . . ." *Daily Mail*, July 31, 2009. http://www.dailymail.co.uk/news/worldnews/article-1203028/Will-Krakatoa-rock-world-Last-time-killed-thousands-changed-weather-years-deadlier.html

Erickson, Jon. *Rock Formations and Unusual Geologic Structures.* New York: Checkmark Books, 2001.

Lawton, Rebecca, Diane Lawton, and Susan Panttaja. *Discover Nature in the Rocks.* Mechanicsburg, PA: Stackpole Books, 1997.

McMenamin, Mark *A.S. Science 101: Geology.* New York: HarperCollins, 2007.

Moseman, Andrew. "Disaster! The Most Destructive Volcanic Eruptions in History." *Discover Magazine,* June 23, 2009. http://discovermagazine.com/photos/23-most-destructive-volcanic-eruptions-in-history

Muir, Hazel. "Science of Mentos–Diet Coke Explosions Explained." *New Scientist*, June 12, 2008. http://www.newscientist.com/article/dn14114-science-of-mentosdiet-coke-explosions-explained.html

Newhall, Chris, James W. Hendley II, and Peter H. Stauffer. "The Cataclysmic 1991 Eruption of Mount Pinatubo, Philippines." United States Geological Survey Fact Sheet, pp. 113-97. http://pubs.usgs.gov/fs/1997/fs113-97/

Radice, Betty (translator). *The Letters of the Younger Pliny.* New York: Penguin Putnam, 1963, 1969.

Riley, C. M. "Tephra." http://www.geo.mtu.edu/volcanoes/hazards/primer/tephra.html

Rosi, Mauro, Paolo Papale, Luca Lupi, and Marco Stoppato. *Volcanoes.* Buffalo, NY: Firefly Books, Inc., 2003.

Smith, Peter J., ed. *The Earth.* New York: Macmillan Publishing Company, 1986.

Smithsonian Institution: Global Volcanism Program. "Worldwide Holocene Volcano and Eruption Information." http://www.volcano.si.edu/

Sutherland, Lin. *The Volcanic Earth.* Sydney, Australia: University of South Wales Press, 1995.

University of California. "Mantle Plume and Hot Spot Stability." *UC Newsroom,* December 5, 2002. http://www.universityofcalifornia.edu/news/article/5015

Wood, Robert Muir. *Earthquakes and Volcanoes.* New York: Weidenfeld & Nicolson, 1987.

Zais, Dick. "Managing the Mt. St. Helens Volcanic Ashfall on Yakima, Washington, U.S.A." Presented at the Cities on Volcanoes 2 Conference, Auckland, New Zealand, February 14, 2001.

On the Internet

Cascades Volcano Observatory
    http://vulcan.wr.usgs.gov/

Federal Emergency Management Agency: Volcanoes for Kids
    http://www.fema.gov/kids/volcano.htm

Michigan Technological University Volcanoes Page
    http://www.geo.mtu.edu/volcanoes/

Oregon State University: Volcano World
    http://volcano.oregonstate.edu/

Smithsonian National Museum of Natural History: The Dynamic Earth
    http://www.mnh.si.edu/earth/main_frames.html

U.S. Department of Energy Kids: Geothermal Energy
    http://tonto.eia.doe.gov/kids/energy.cfm?page=geothermal_home-basics

U.S. Geological Survey: Hawaiian Volcano Observatory
    http://hvo.wr.usgs.gov/

GLOSSARY

ash—Microscopic particles from burning wood or volcanic explosions.

asthenosphere (as-THEN-oh-sfeer)—Region of the Earth's upper mantle just below the lithosphere, made of rock so hot that it can slowly flow.

basalt (buh-SALT)—A black volcanic rock.

caustic (KOS-tik)—Burning or corroding to living tissues.

cinder cone—A type of volcano with steep sides that forms around a vent. Examples include Sunset Crater in Arizona and Cerro Negro in Nicaragua.

core—The innermost layer of the earth, made of iron and nickel. It has a thick, liquid outer core and a solid inner core.

crust—The outermost layer of the earth, where all geology that humans can see occurs.

felsic (FEL-sik)—Enriched with minerals made from silicon and oxygen. Felsic magmas are the most explosive because their high viscosity traps water and gases.

fissure (FISH-ur)—Crack or hole caused by breaking.

gas—The most excited state of matter. Air is a gas.

geothermal (jee-oh-THER-mul) **power**—Using the heat of the earth to boil water, which turns a turbine to generate electricity.

hot spot—A fixed place in the mantle where the asthenosphere brings much hotter magma very close to the lithosphere.

igneous (IG-nee-us) **rock**—Rock derived directly from cooled magma or lava.

lahar (lay-HAR)—A flow of mud and volcanic debris.

lapilli (la-PIL-eye)—Pebble-sized volcanic debris. Meaning "little stones" in Latin.

lava (LAH-vuh)—Molten rock that comes to the earth's surface during a volcanic eruption.

lava bomb—Piece of lava greater than 2.5 inches (64 millimeters) in diameter, shot out of a volcano during an explosive eruption.

lithosphere (LITH-oh-sfeer)—Outermost layer of the earth containing the continental and oceanic plates.

magma (MAG-muh)—The mixture of molten rock, solid crystals, and gases that makes up the earth's mantle.

mantle—Thick, hot layer of partially molten rock under the lithosphere.

plate—Continent-sized pieces of the lithosphere.

plate tectonics (tek-TAH-niks)—Geologic theory suggesting that the continents and oceans are made of huge rafts of rock. The rafts, or plates, move very slowly on currents of magma in the asthenosphere below.

plutonic (ploo-TAH-nik) **rock**—Igneous rock that formed inside the earth.

principle of superposition—Geologic law which states that, in a stack of layered earth materials, the bottom layers are older than the top ones.

rhyolite (RY-oh-lyt)—Light-colored (felsic) volcanic rock.

shield volcano—A volcano with gently sloping sides, made from low-viscosity lava flows. Examples include Skjaldbreidur in Iceland and Mauna Loa in Hawaii.

stratovolcano (STRAT-oh-vol-kay-noh)—A tall, cone-shaped volcano built from many layers of lava and tephra. Examples include Mt. St. Helens in Washington and Krakatoa in Indonesia.

subduction zone—Area where one tectonic plate is forced under another.

surface tension—The strength of a liquid's surface, determined by interactions between molecules in the liquid.

tephra (TEF-rah)—Debris ejected from a volcano.

tiltmeter—Instrument that measures changes in the slope of the ground, especially near a volcano to monitor an impending eruption.

viscous (VIS-kus)—Resistant to flow. Highly viscous liquids flow slowly; low **viscosity** liquids flow quickly.

volcanology (vul-kun-AH-luh-jee)—A branch of geology devoted to the study of volcanoes.

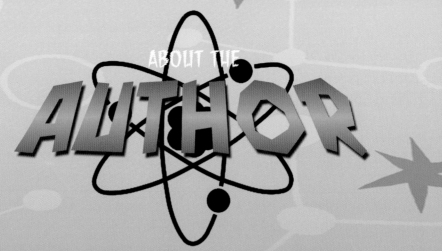

ABOUT THE AUTHOR

Claire O'Neal has written over a dozen books for Mitchell Lane Publishers, including *A Project Guide to Rocks and Minerals* and *A Project Guide to Earthquakes* for this series, and *Projects in Genetics* and *Exploring Earth's Biomes* in the series Life Science Projects for Kids. She holds degrees in English and biology from Indiana University, and a Ph.D. in chemistry from the University of Washington. She lived in the shadow of Mt. Rainier for five years. Now she makes her home in Delaware, where it is tectonically boring, with her geologist husband and two young sons.